Growing Together
Marriage Enrichment for Every Culture

Workbook

DR. BOB ABRAMSON

Alphabet Resources

Growing Together - Marriage Enrichment for Every Culture - Workbook
Published by Alphabet Resources, Inc.
365 Stonehenge Drive
Phillipsburg, NJ 08865
1-561-963-0778
Dr.Bob@mentoringministry.com or BNAbramson@aol.com

Cover design by Ryan Stacey

10 digit ISBN 0-9843443-5-7
13 digit ISBN 978-0-9843443-5-2

Library of Congress Control Number 2010936223

Contact Dr. Abramson by visiting
www.mentoringministry.com
or
Dr.Bob@mentoringministry.com

This workbook is designed to compliment *"Growing Together."* Its intent is to help you understand, reflect on and implement the principles found in the book. It is not intended to stand alone. The questions and exercises require the reader to work with the book. This workbook may be used by couples, for individual study or group discussion.

৯০৩৯০৩৯০৩৯০৩৯০৩৯০৩৯০৩৯০৩৯০৩৯০৩৯০৩৯০৩		
CONTENTS		
PART 1		
INTRODUCTION		3
1.	GOD'S VIEW OF MARRIAGE	5
2.	HUSBAND AND WIFE: DIFFERENT BY GOD'S DELIBERATE DESIGN	13
3.	MARITAL LOVE: GOD'S DWELLING PLACE FOR YOU	19
4.	COMMUNICATION: SPEAKING THE TRUTH IN LOVE	25
5.	YOUR PRIVATE GARDENS: TWO PLACES OF INTIMACY FROM GOD	32
PART 2		
6.	WHAT IS LOVE?	45
7.	TENDER MERCIES	55
8.	TRUSTING HEARTS	63
9.	FOR THE GLORY OF GOD	71
৯০৩৯০৩৯০৩৯০৩৯০৩৯০৩৯০৩৯০৩৯০৩৯০৩৯০৩৯০		

INTRODUCTION

On Page 2 of the introduction to his book, *"Growing Together,"* Dr. Abramson writes the following.

> *"Growing Together"* provides you with information about how to nourish and enrich your marriage. It is designed to be read together by husband and wife. It will challenge both of you to take your marriage to places of richness, great joy, satisfaction and fruitfulness. It can also be of great interest to those who are contemplating marriage, or simply want to learn more about God's design for the marriage relationship.
>
> *"Growing Together"* is intended to cross Christian denominational lines and work in every culture. It explores ways to enrich Christian marriage, regardless of cultural setting and context. It works equally well for single-culture and cross-cultural marriages… It will give you guidance on how to go about enriching your marriage God's way.
>
> I have written *"Growing Together"* from a Christian viewpoint. The principles you will discover in the book are universal. They have their foundations in God's completely dependable Word."
>
> *(2 Timothy 3:16 NKJV) "All Scripture is given by inspiration of God, and is profitable for doctrine, for reproof, for correction, for instruction in righteousness,"*

This workbook can be used by individuals, couples working together, or in a group setting. If you are doing this as an individual or couple, you are now ready to proceed to the first chapter. Read Chapter 1 of *"Growing Together."* Do the assignments you will find on Pages 5-12 of this workbook. If you are part of a group, read and observe the instructions regarding basic boundaries on the next page, before proceeding to Page 5.

BASIC BOUNDARIES FOR GROUP DISCUSSIONS

1. All groups using this workbook will be divided by gender, men with men only, and women with women only.
2. **Never** share anything personal about your husband or wife. This workbook is about discovering what **you** can do to enrich your marriage.
3. Protect the confidentiality and trust within the group. **Do not** share any part of the group discussions with anyone outside of your group.
4. You are encouraged to share your own workbook information with your spouse.

When the group is formed, do the following.

Introduce yourselves to each other. Tell a little bit about your backgrounds and how long you have been married.

1. Share what comes to mind as <u>the best thing</u> about your marriage.
2. Share what you might want your marriage to grow into, as a result of this series of studies, exercises and discussions. Remember, this workbook is to aid you in enriching your marriage. Always focus on the positives.

Chapter 1 - GOD'S VIEW OF MARRIAGE

Marriage can be a puzzle. What do you think are three core principles of marriage enrichment? Each piece of the puzzle below represents a core principle. Begin with a first attempt at filling in the puzzle diagram below. Write one core principle in each of the puzzle pieces, using no more than three words for each principle. For now, limit your answers to three core principles. We will add more pieces to the puzzle later.

Core Principles of Marriage Enrichment

1.   2.   3.

Discuss the labels for your three puzzle pieces with your spouse, facilitator and group. Then list five more core principles that members of your group suggested that are different from yours. List them in order of how you perceive them, in importance to you.

4. _____

5. _____

6. _____

7. _____

8. _____

On Page 5 of *"Growing Together,"* Dr. Abramson writes the following:

> *""Growing Together"* will give you insight into ways to enrich your marriage. God wants a very real part in designing your relationship as husband and wife. He wants you to have an even better life, and will help you build on the good things you already share in your marriage experience."

List in one short sentence each, in the order of their importance to <u>you</u>, the three most important things in your marriage.

1.

_____

2.

_____

3.

_____

If in a group, compare your answers with those of the others in your group. When you are <u>alone with your spouse</u>, discuss and compare your answers.

On Page 6 of *"Growing Together,"* you will find this illustration of how God sees marriage.

_____

GOD'S VIEW OF MARRIAGE
☑ ONE FLESH
☑ A COVENANT AGREEMENT
☑ A PARTNERSHIP

_____

ONE FLESH IS A GOD IDEA

(Genesis 2:24 NKJV) "Therefore a man shall leave his father and mother and be joined to his wife, and they shall become one flesh."

In two or three sentences each, give your opinion about what the three elements of God's view of marriage mean. Write from your heart, not from what you might arrive at from anyone else's opinion.

☑ ONE FLESH

_____
_____
_____
_____
_____

☑ A COVENANT AGREEMENT

_____
_____
_____
_____
_____

☑ A PARTNERSHIP

_____
_____
_____
_____

1. Discuss your opinions, above, with your spouse.
2. When you are in your group, discuss your opinions with your facilitator and group. (Remember our basic boundaries for group discussions. Do not share anything personal about your husband or wife.)

Work with your group to try to get agreement on what these three terms mean. While in your group, record on the following page, what you have agreed upon.

☑ ONE FLESH (Group opinion)

_____
_____
_____
_____
_____

☑ A COVENANT AGREEMENT (Group opinion)

_____
_____
_____
_____
_____

☑ A PARTNERSHIP (Group opinion)

_____
_____
_____
_____
_____

On Page 8 of *"Growing Together,"* you will find the following:

> "The foundation of marriage is not romance or emotion, but a rock-solid commitment to a covenant. If we believe our commitments to Christ and to the kingdom of God are covenant commitments, we will see our obligation to the person we are married to as a direct expression of these commitments."

God sees you and your spouse as one, working together in agreement in a partnership. In God's eyes, your marriage vows were declarations of covenant. Your words not only obligated you to your marriage partner, but also to God. He is the third Partner in your covenant marriage agreement. Discuss this with your spouse, facilitator and group.

MARRIAGE: A PARTNERSHIP OF GRACE

(Genesis 2:18 NKJV) "And the LORD God said, "It is not good that man should be alone; I will make him a helper comparable to him.""

On Pages 9 and 10 of *"Growing Together,"* you will find the following:

"In Genesis 2:18, God did not say, *"I will make him another exactly like him."* The Lord said, *"I will make him a helper, comparable to him."* God intended both husband and wife to be equal in worth, in His eyes and in the eyes of each other."

(Romans 2:11 NKJV) "For there is no partiality with God."

"Scripture clearly teaches that God treats everyone the same. We are to follow the example of the Lord and not look down upon others. How much more should this truth be applied in our marriages? We are to see each other as God sees us. We are partners with different responsibilities and tasks, but equal in His sight. Our actions are to be a reflection of this truth. This may require a serious change in our attitudes."

In every society, there are gender-specific cultural prejudices. You may have been raised to witness these and perhaps embraced some of them. Romans 2:11 teaches us that God has no prejudice. The Bible says that you and your spouse are equal in His eyes. You do have different tasks and responsibilities. You do have differing authority in the home. Think about whether any of your attitudes need to be modified or rejected, so they will align with biblical teaching. Discuss this subject with your spouse, your facilitator and group.

On the following page, list some of the most prevalent prejudices and wrong attitudes that may negatively affect marriages.

Prejudices and wrong attitudes that may negatively affect marriage:

_____

_____

_____

_____

_____

_____

_____

_____

_____

_____

_____

_____

On Page 11 of *"Growing Together,"* you will find the following:

YOUR MARRIAGE WILL ONLY BE SUCCESSFUL
AND ENRICHING TO THE DEGREE THAT YOU
ALLOW GOD'S GRACE TO FLOW THROUGH IT.

At the bottom of Page 11 and continuing on Page 12 of *"Growing Together,"* you read the following definition of grace. Carefully look at it again:

"Grace is the goodness of God, stored up in heaven, just waiting for your willingness to allow it to flow through you to your spouse. Your willingness in action can be called real love - God's kind of love."

Page 12 of *"Growing Together"* illustrates this definition. →

GRACE

REAL
LOVE

BLESSINGS

10.

Does your relationship currently allow this definition of grace to be a driving force in your marriage? Discuss this with your spouse, facilitator and group. Come to agreement on an expanded, amplified version of this definition. Write it in the space below. (Remember our basic boundaries for group discussions. Do not share anything personal about your husband or wife.)

_____

_____

_____

_____

_____

_____

_____

_____

On Page 12 of *"Growing Together,"* you read the following definition of "Real Love." Carefully look at it again:

> "Real love is your deliberate, active, living effort to bring to your marriage partner, as much of God's grace as possible, at whatever the cost to you. Real love is seen in the flow of God's grace through you to your spouse."

After considering what you have covered in this first chapter, now add and label a fourth core principle piece to your puzzle.

Core Principles of Marriage Enrichment

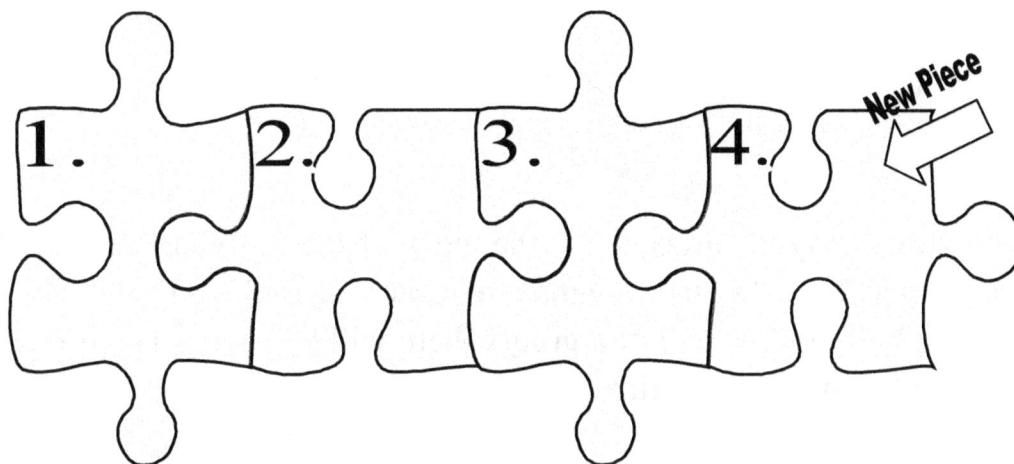

"Growing Together" makes the connection between grace and "real love." Now it is up to you to make the same connection for your marriage. End this chapter with a group discussion of this vital connection. Record the most prominent and challenging thoughts that Chapter 1 brought to you.

_____

_____

_____

_____

_____

_____

_____

_____

_____

_____

_____

_____

_____

_____

_____

_____

_____

_____

_____

_____

_____

_____

You are now ready to proceed to the next chapter. Read Chapter 2 of *"Growing Together."* Do the assignments you will find on Pages 14-18 of this workbook. If you are part of a group, there will be additional parts of the workbook to fill in at the meeting.

Chapter 2 - HUSBAND AND WIFE: DIFFERENT BY GOD'S DELIBERATE DESIGN

(Genesis 2:15 NKJV) "Then the LORD God took the man and put him in the garden of Eden to tend and keep it."

UNDERSTANDING THE DIFFERENCES BETWEEN "DOING" AND "BEING"

Consider the following excerpts from the beginning of this chapter. Pay special attention to the thoughts that are shown in bold type.

Page 14 (second paragraph): "Men are built to show love by actions that may seem unrelated to the intimate expressions of love their wives want. **This can lead to misunderstanding and feelings of sadness or loss by their wives.** They may feel their husbands do not care about them as they should."

Page 15: "In many marriages, a woman spends so much time working, that she and her husband lack time together. **He may take it as a signal that she would rather be away from him.** This misunderstanding may cause him to hold back his affections. He might fail to see she is emotionally in need of him expressing his love to her. As a result, she will feel she is taken for granted. She too will feel the loneliness and rejection he feels. **Consequently, there will seldom (or perhaps never) be any true, meaningful closeness.**"

Let's look closely at the underlined portions below.

1. "This can lead to <u>misunderstanding</u> and <u>feelings of sadness or loss</u> by their wives."
2. "He may take it as <u>a signal</u> that <u>she would rather be away from him</u>."
3. "Consequently, there will seldom (or perhaps never) be any true, <u>meaningful closeness</u>."

Consider the following chart. Discuss it with your spouse, facilitator and group.

1.	Misunderstanding, feelings of sadness or loss	1.	Understanding, feelings of joy and great gain
2.	Rather be away (apart)	2.	Rather be nearby
3.	Lack of meaningful closeness	3.	Meaningful closeness (one flesh)

Below, list one action for each of the three points in the left side of the chart that <u>you have the power to change</u>, and that would move some vulnerable part of your relationship from the left column toward the right column.

	Issues		Actions I can take
1.	Misunderstanding, feelings of sadness or loss	1.	
2.	Rather be away (apart)	2.	
3.	Lack of meaningful closeness	3.	

Discuss what you wrote concerning your three actions in the chart above with your spouse, facilitator and group. (Remember, **do not share anything that would embarrass your marriage partner**. This is about actions <u>you</u> can take.)

Below, record anything in the group discussion that particularly touched your heart, and convinced you to consider changing some of the ways you relate to your spouse.

_____

_____

_____

_____

_____

OUR ATTITUDES AND ACTIONS
(God's Foolproof Formula for Marriage Enrichment)
(Pages 17 and 18 of *"Growing Together"*)

(Ephesians 5:22-24 NKJV) "<u>Wives, submit to your own husbands, as to the Lord.</u> {23} For the husband is the head of the wife, as also Christ is head of the church; and He is the Savior of the body. {24} Therefore, just as the church is subject to Christ, so let the wives be to their own husbands in everything."

(Ephesians 5:25, 28-29 NKJV) "<u>Husbands,</u> love your wives, just as Christ also loved the church and gave Himself for her... {28} So husbands ought to love their own wives as their own bodies; he who loves his wife loves himself {29} For no one ever hated his own flesh, <u>but nourishes and cherishes it, just as the Lord does the church.</u>"

TO NOURISH IS TO FEED ANOTHER SO THEY WILL GROW IN HEALTH AND BECOME STRONG.

TO CHERISH IS TO VALUE TO AN EXTREME; TO HOLD DEARLY; TO WATCH OVER LOVINGLY.

CAUSE (Leads to →)	EFFECT
☑ Wives, submit to your own husband, as to the Lord.	Marriage Enrichment ☑ One flesh
☑ Husbands, love your own wife as your own body. ☑ Nourish and cherish your wife just as the Lord does the church.	☑ Strong covenant bindings ☑ A successful, highly significant, joyful and peaceful partnership

Discuss the cause and effect chart on the previous page with your spouse, facilitator and group. From your discussions, add additional effects of the heavenly instructions of Ephesians 5.

_____

_____

_____

_____

_____

_____

_____

_____

_____

_____

Now look at these four points from Page 19 of *"Growing Together."*

- ☑ Husbands, look to the Cross for your example of love.
- ☑ Wives, look to Christ. He is your example of submission.
- ☑ Look for the love of God in each other.
- ☑ Honor Christ by submitting to each other.

When you add these to the cause and effect chart on the previous page, you have a fine start on understanding a supernaturally enabled and enriched marriage. Which do you think is the most difficult of these four points for any marriage? Why?

_____

_____

_____

_____

_____

_____

Discuss this with your spouse, facilitator and group.

TAKE INVENTORY: YOUR NEEDS ARE DIFFERENT BY DESIGN
(Pages 20-22 of *"Growing Together"*)

On Page 21 of *"Growing Together,"* you were asked to take inventory of the list, titled, "I HAVE NOT GIVEN MY SPOUSE..." You were offered sixteen possible things you may not be giving to your spouse. There was an additional space for a seventeenth item of your choosing.

1. Think about what is on this list, or what would fit in the seventeenth item. Pick what you most want to give your spouse that you have not been willing or able to give yet. Discuss this with your spouse, your facilitator and group. (Remember our basic boundaries for group discussions. Do not share anything personal about your husband or wife.)

2. Paying special attention to the item on the list labeled "Honor," do the following exercise.

HONOR

Answer the following <u>without looking at Page 27</u> of *"Growing Together."*
What is honor?

_____

_____

_____

_____

Why is giving honor to our spouses vital to marriage enrichment?

_____

_____

_____

_____

_____

Husbands: Look again at Page 27 of *"Growing Together,"* and review what was written about giving your wife honor. Discuss this with your spouse, facilitator and group.

WHAT DOES EVERY MAN NEED FROM HIS WIFE?
WHAT DOES EVERY WOMAN NEED FROM HER HUSBAND?

Spend time reading Pages 22-27 with your spouse. In the space below, agree on, and record something constructive that came from doing so together.

_____

_____

_____

_____

_____

_____

_____

_____

As we close Chapter 2, be sure to read the poems on Pages 29-31 with your spouse. Have a discussion with your spouse, facilitator and group about the impact this chapter had on you.

You are now ready to proceed to the next chapter. Read Chapter 3 of *"Growing Together."* Do the assignments you will find on Pages 19-24 of this workbook. If you are part of a group, there will be additional parts of the workbook to fill in at the meeting.

Chapter 3 - MARITAL LOVE: GOD'S DWELLING PLACE FOR YOU

Look again at your puzzle diagram of the core principles of marriage enrichment (Workbook, Page 11). If you want to change any puzzle labels, do so now. Using the puzzle below, consider what you have covered in the second chapter. Label the fifth core principle piece, added to your puzzle.

Core Principles of Marriage Enrichment

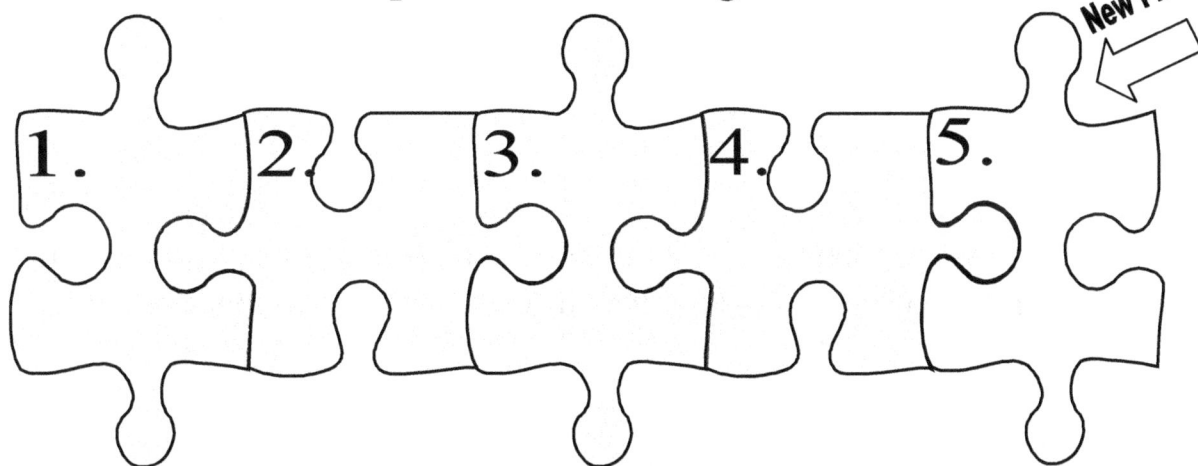

New Piece

1. 2. 3. 4. 5.

Discuss the puzzle with your spouse first, then with your facilitator and group. Listen to what others in the group have in their puzzles. After doing so, everyone agree on a group-defined puzzle. Fill it in below.

Core Principles of Marriage Enrichment (Group)

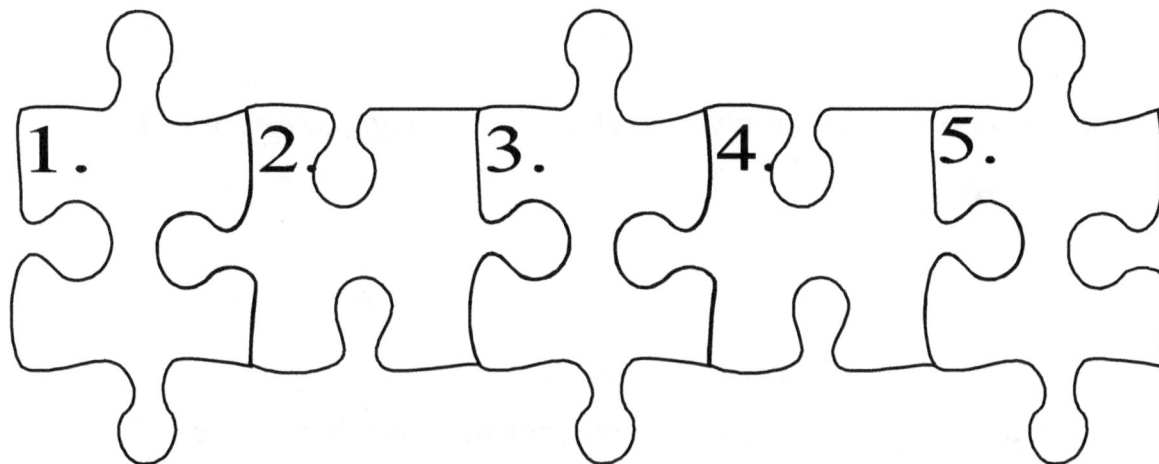

1. 2. 3. 4. 5.

List the five pieces of the group's puzzle.

1. _____

2. _____

3. _____

4. _____

5. _____

Is there much disagreement between your five pieces and the group's? Did any of the group's pieces give you difficulty? If so, list these below and briefly explain why you could not include them in your own puzzle.

_____

_____

_____

_____

Did the group's puzzle cause you to change your own puzzle? Why?

_____

_____

_____

If you made any changes, be sure to re-label your puzzle on Page 19.

Here are THE SEVEN BIBLICAL PILLARS OF LOVE, from 1 Corinthians 13:4-7 (Page 35 of *"Growing Together"*).

1. LOVE IS PATIENT.
2. LOVE IS KIND.
3. LOVE REJOICES IN THE TRUTH.
4. LOVE ALWAYS PROTECTS.
5. LOVE ALWAYS TRUSTS.
6. LOVE ALWAYS HOPES.
7. LOVE ALWAYS PERSEVERES.

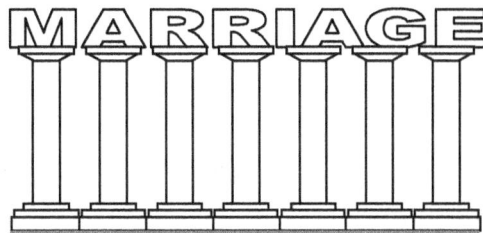

Answer the following questions related to these seven pillars.

1. What would you say is the primary cause of impatience in a relationship?

_____

_____

_____

_____

2. What would you say typically causes unkind thoughts in a relationship?

_____

_____

_____

_____

3. How important is truth to your marriage?

_____

_____

_____

_____

4. What should you be most protective of concerning your spouse's feelings?

_____

_____

_____

_____

5. What one thing commonly generates undeserved mistrust between spouses?

_____

_____

_____

_____

6. What is the greatest hope you have for your marriage? Be as specific as you can.

_____

_____

_____

_____

7. What would you say is the most prominent emotion that threatens the marriage covenant and the determination to persevere and honor it?

_____

_____

_____

_____

Discuss these seven questions with your spouse, facilitator and group. Listen to what others have to say. In the space below, reflect on how your answers, your spouse's answers and your group's answers have challenged your thinking.

_____

_____

_____

_____

_____

_____

_____

_____

_____

Now that you have gone through the seven pillars individually, and then with your spouse and group, look again at Dr. Abramson's definition of real love (Page 11 of the workbook and Page 34 of *"Growing Together"*).

> "Real love is your deliberate, active, living effort to bring to your marriage partner, as much of God's grace as possible, at whatever the cost to you. Real love is seen in the flow of God's grace through you to your spouse."

Take the time to reflect on one specific behavioral change that deliberately and actively could enrich most relationships. Discuss it in the space below. Explain why this change would enrich your relationship. Share your answer with your spouse, your facilitator and group.

_____

_____

_____

_____

_____

_____

_____

_____

Reflect on the part of the definition of "real love" that said, "…whatever the cost to you." Record your thoughts below.

_____

_____

_____

_____

_____

_____

_____

_____

As this section of the workbook closes, consider again, the words at bottom of Page 41 of *"Growing Together."*

> "These seven pillars, working together, will give you every opportunity to dwell in a loving, enriched, fruitful and satisfying marriage."

Share your thoughts on these words with your spouse, facilitator and group. Record anything significant to the subject of marriage enrichment that touched your heart in a special way.

_____

_____

_____

_____

_____

_____

_____

_____

_____

_____

_____

_____

_____

_____

_____

_____

_____

_____

You are now ready to proceed to the next chapter. Read Chapter 4 of *"Growing Together."* Do the assignments you will find on Pages 25-32 of this workbook. If you are part of a group, there will be additional parts of the workbook to fill in at the meeting.

Chapter 4 - COMMUNICATION: SPEAKING THE TRUTH IN LOVE

(The Language of Biblical Closeness)

In the puzzle below, fill in your latest labels from Page 19.

Core Principles of Marriage Enrichment

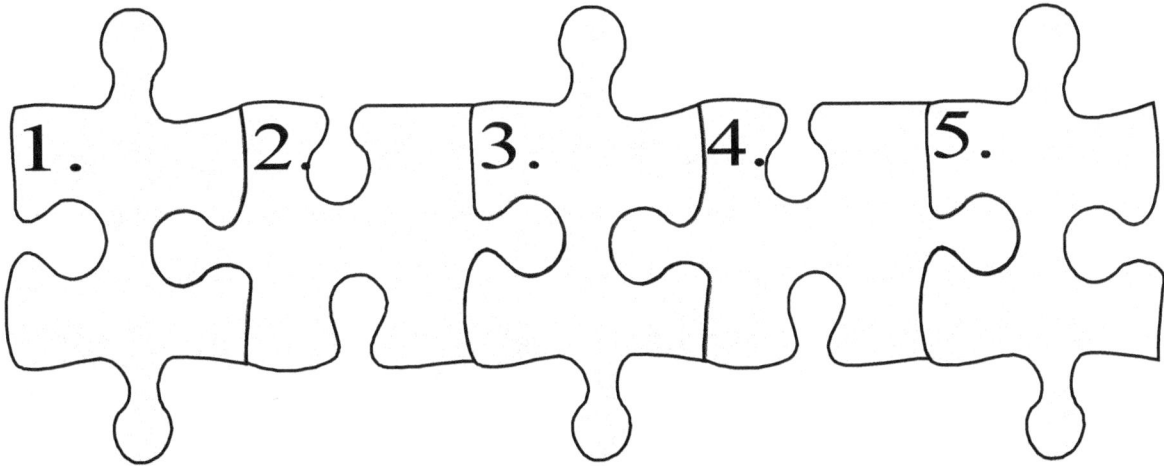

1.
2.
3.
4.
5.

Chapter 4 of *"Growing Together"* begins with the following:

(Ephesians 4:15 NKJV) "…speaking the truth in love, may grow up in all things into Him who is the head; Christ;"

"The key ingredient to understanding each other is to communicate lovingly and truthfully. Learning to speak the truth in love more willingly and more often will enrich your relationship as husband and wife."

What stops you from speaking the truth in love?

The bottom of Page 44 of *"Growing Together"* asks, "WHAT STOPS YOU FROM SPEAKING THE TRUTH IN LOVE?" This section of the book teaches that the primary reason we do not always speak lovingly and truthfully is because of our attitudes. Notice the order of the three attitudes given: (1) towards God, (2) towards His Word, and (3) towards each other. The order is important. How you order your attitudes will affect your heart, and in turn, how you speak. Your attitude toward God ought to be your highest priority, even higher than to your spouse. Keeping your words accountable to God and honoring His Word will cause what you say to be full of love, truth and grace. These first two attitudes guarantee the third, which is a good attitude toward each other. This is a foundational principle for marriage enrichment.

Look at your puzzle on the previous page. Do any of your labels contradict Ephesians 4:15 and the "key ingredient" of communicating lovingly and truthfully? If so, consider whether you need to modify or even change any of the labels. Discuss any changes you make with your spouse, facilitator and group.

Core Principles of Marriage Enrichment

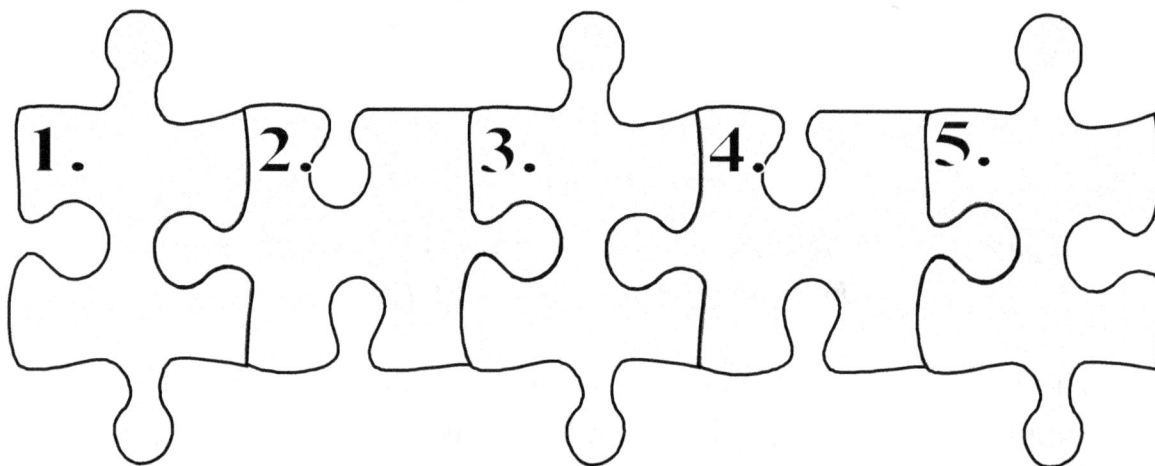

1.   2.   3.   4.   5.

What helps you speak the truth in love?

(Ephesians 4:23 NKJV) "And be renewed in the spirit of your mind."

To be renewed means to tear down and rebuild. This relates to our attitudes, referred to on Page 45 of *"Growing Together"* as "the patterns of our thinking." What is there about your communication between each other that needs to be renewed (demolished and rebuilt) in a better, stronger way?

_____

_____

_____

_____

_____

_____

Practical Steps to Truthful and Loving Communication
(Pages 46-55 of *"Growing Together"*)

(Ephesians 4:3 NKJV) "endeavoring to keep the unity of the Spirit in the bond of peace."

First Step

"Bring the unity of the Spirit and the bond of peace into your speech and therefore, into your relationship."

This first step is taken from Ephesians 4:3. It emphasizes an active effort to guard spiritual unity and hold it together with peace. Two warnings are given. On Page 47 of *"Growing Together,"* it says to first, avoid lies. Is it ever permissible for one spouse to lie to the other? Write your answer below, and then share it with your spouse, facilitator and group. (Remember our basic boundaries for group discussions. Do not share anything personal about your husband or wife.)

_____

_____

_____

_____

_____

_____

27.

Second, the book says not to let your anger go unresolved. Anger, if not addressed, leads to bitterness, which poisons your relationship. Choose the most typical way you handle anger from the three categories below and explain. Be honest with yourself.

1. Blow up

_____

2. Clam up (stuff it inside)

_____

3. Surrender it to God.

_____

Biblically speaking, the answer to anger is always to surrender it to God. Do you need to change how you handle anger? In your group, discuss what it means to surrender something to God.

Second Step

Learn to give gifts to your marriage partner.

This is not about birthday gifts or Christmas presents, though these can certainly be wonderful gifts to each other. Review Page 48 of *"Growing Together."* Comment on which gift mentioned there touches your heart the most. If you want, write about another gift that touches your heart even more than the four you read about in the book.

_____
_____
_____
_____
_____
_____

Compare your thoughts on giving gifts with your spouse, facilitator and group. (Remember our basic boundaries for group discussions. Do not share anything personal about your husband or wife.)

Third Step

Learn to listen.

This is one of those critical places in *"Growing Together"* that calls for increased attention. The sequences described on Pages 49-55 are perhaps the most vital pieces of information for any couple to embrace and practice. Carefully review the sequence shown in the diagram below.

CARNAL LISTENING

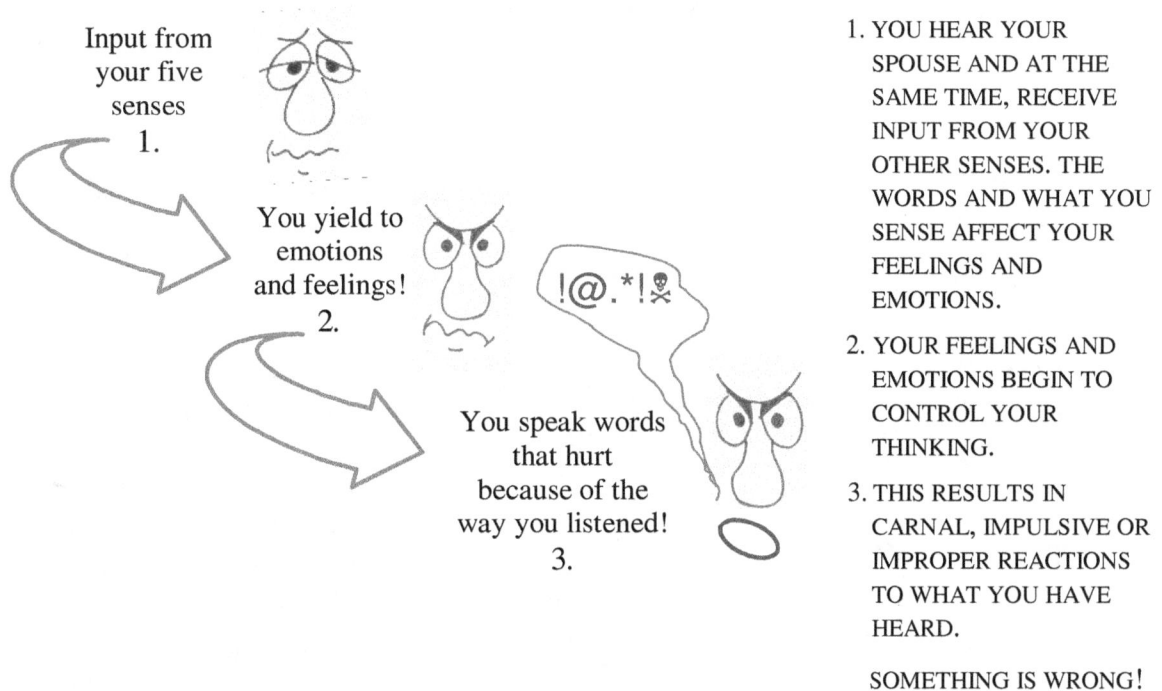

Input from your five senses
1.

You yield to emotions and feelings!
2.

You speak words that hurt because of the way you listened!
3.

!@.*!☠

1. YOU HEAR YOUR SPOUSE AND AT THE SAME TIME, RECEIVE INPUT FROM YOUR OTHER SENSES. THE WORDS AND WHAT YOU SENSE AFFECT YOUR FEELINGS AND EMOTIONS.

2. YOUR FEELINGS AND EMOTIONS BEGIN TO CONTROL YOUR THINKING.

3. THIS RESULTS IN CARNAL, IMPULSIVE OR IMPROPER REACTIONS TO WHAT YOU HAVE HEARD.

SOMETHING IS WRONG!

On Page 51 of *"Growing Together,"* Dr. Abramson writes the following.

"Carnal listening allows no room for God, but forces you to operate from the place of your emotions. There is nowhere in the sequence to stop and seek guidance from the Holy Spirit. Misunderstanding and impulsive reaction then causes division and strife. Things begin to spiral out of control. Since you no longer exercise control over your feelings or actions, peace is replaced by strife. The basis for your relationship is eroded. In some measure, your covenant marriage partnership will be weakened and you grow apart from each other."

Look again, at what you wrote in the chart on Page 28 on the three ways to handle anger. Blowing up and clamming up relate directly to our diagram on carnal listening (previous page). Do your responses to anger typically match that diagram? Handling anger correctly by surrendering it to God can be a powerful tool for marriage enrichment. Now look at the correct and fruitful way to listen.

"LISTENING AFTER THE SPIRIT"
(THE RIGHT WAY TO LISTEN)

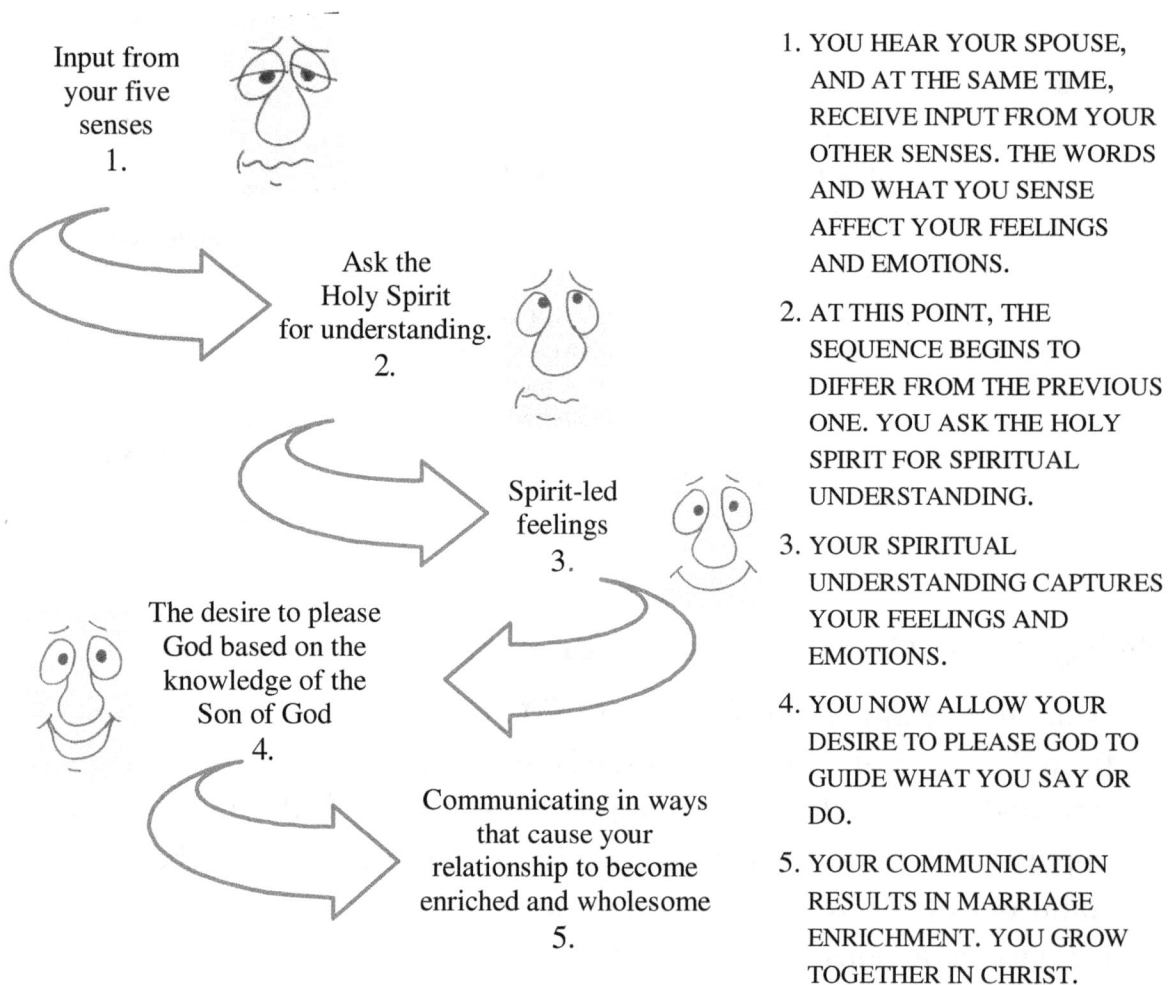

Input from
your five
senses
1.

Ask the
Holy Spirit
for understanding.
2.

Spirit-led
feelings
3.

The desire to please
God based on the
knowledge of the
Son of God
4.

Communicating in ways
that cause your
relationship to become
enriched and wholesome
5.

1. YOU HEAR YOUR SPOUSE, AND AT THE SAME TIME, RECEIVE INPUT FROM YOUR OTHER SENSES. THE WORDS AND WHAT YOU SENSE AFFECT YOUR FEELINGS AND EMOTIONS.

2. AT THIS POINT, THE SEQUENCE BEGINS TO DIFFER FROM THE PREVIOUS ONE. YOU ASK THE HOLY SPIRIT FOR SPIRITUAL UNDERSTANDING.

3. YOUR SPIRITUAL UNDERSTANDING CAPTURES YOUR FEELINGS AND EMOTIONS.

4. YOU NOW ALLOW YOUR DESIRE TO PLEASE GOD TO GUIDE WHAT YOU SAY OR DO.

5. YOUR COMMUNICATION RESULTS IN MARRIAGE ENRICHMENT. YOU GROW TOGETHER IN CHRIST.

Some of the most vital pieces of information for any couple to embrace and practice are found in understanding the two diagrams on listening. Consider how you and your spouse communicate. What could change?

_____

_____

_____

_____

Share your thoughts with your spouse, facilitator and group. (Remember our basic boundaries for group discussions. Do not share anything personal about your husband or wife.)

FORGIVENESS: ARE YOU WILLING? GOD WAS.

Chapter 4 concludes with the issue of forgiveness. Effective and true forgiveness begins in the heart. If forgiveness is going to make a difference between spouses, it must be communicated through words and actions.

Are there patterns of thinking or behavior in your life that make it difficult to forgive? Search your heart. Do any of these manifest themselves toward your spouse on far too regular a basis? Conclude by filling out the chart below. Be honest and transparent with yourself.

Patterns of Wrong Behavior:	Remedy:

Share your thoughts with your spouse, facilitator and group. (Remember our basic boundaries for group discussions. Do not share anything personal about your husband or wife.)

You are now ready to proceed to the next chapter. Read Chapter 5 of "Growing Together." Do the assignments you will find on Pages 33-41 of this workbook. If you are part of a group, there will be additional parts of the workbook to fill in at the meeting.

Chapter 5 - YOUR PRIVATE GARDENS: TWO PLACES OF INTIMACY FROM GOD

(Song of Solomon 5:1a NKJV) *"I have come to my garden, my sister, my spouse;"*

Scripture identifies a wife in three ways.

- YOUR GARDEN
- YOUR SISTER
- YOUR SPOUSE

Husbands: What does each of these mean for your attitudes toward your wife?

She is your garden:

_____

_____

She is your sister:

_____

_____

She is your spouse:

_____

_____

Wives: What does each of these mean for your attitudes toward your husband?

You are his garden:

_____

_____

He is your brother:

_____

_____

_____

He is your spouse:

_____

_____

Share your thoughts with your spouse, facilitator and group. (Remember our basic boundaries for group discussions. Do not share anything personal about your husband or wife.)

On Page 60 of *"Growing Together,"* you read the following:

> "No lock will open easily, if it is rusted from being unused or exposed to the wrong elements. The locks on our private gardens need to yield easily. What could cause them to freeze up or become unyielding? Perhaps a person's upbringing, wrong information, fear, or experience influences how he or she looks at sex. Some have a sense of shame. Others feel that sex is something dirty, unlovely or to be endured without joy. God designed sex to be a beautiful, mutually submissive experience."

Your Private Garden

One of the principle issues with a garden is controlling and eliminating weeds. Every garden fights a battle against this unwelcome, unhealthy invasion. If ignored and left alone, weeds eventually dominate and control, as they destroy the beauty of the garden. In the space below, write about what you consider the two most dangerous weeds that might invade a typical private marriage garden. Be sure to explain why you think these are so dangerous.

Most dangerous weed: _____

_____

_____

Second most dangerous weed: _____

_____

_____

Share your thoughts with your spouse, facilitator and group (Remember our basic boundaries for group discussions. Do not share anything personal about your husband or wife.) As a group, what would you agree is the most dangerous weed in a private marriage garden?

_____

_____

_____

_____

Your Sister - Your Brother

At the bottom of Page 60 of *"Growing Together,"* you read the following:

> "Your wife is entitled to all the politeness, deference, care, honor and assistance you would give any woman, who is one of your sisters in Christ. In your particular garden, she is also your wife. How much greater should your watchfulness and care for her be? Be aware of the delicate nature of her feelings. Nurture her. Love her as Christ loves the church."

Notice these terms: "politeness, deference, care, honor and assistance." *"Growing Together"* presents them in the context of writing about the wife. However, they are equally as valid and instructional when a wife considers her husband. Let's focus on the word "deference." The dictionary defines it as, "respectful or courteous regard."[1] Break it down further and the word "respectful" pops out. Ask yourself if your attitudes toward your spouse in your intimate private garden are described by and deserve the word "respectful." Look again at the quote from Page 60, above. The words, "politeness, deference, care, honor and assistance" all work far better when they are done in a "respectful" way.

---

[1] Eurofield Information Solutions Word Genius Dictionary, incorporating Random House Webster's College Dictionary content

How can a couple continually increase their respect for each other in their private, intimate garden? If you share any thoughts with your facilitator and group regarding this question, be sure to protect the privacy of your own garden.

_____

_____

_____

_____

Your Spouse

On Page 61, your read this of a Proverbs 31 wife, "Treat her in ways that show you understand her value and the close-knit connection God has established between the two of you." This principle is the same for both marriage partners. The key word here is value. Ask yourself, how much value and worth do you regularly, routinely place on your spouse, as your gift from God? (No clichés, please. Be honest with yourself.) Write your thoughts, below. Share them with your spouse, facilitator and group. (Remember our basic boundaries for group discussions. Do not share anything personal about your husband or wife.)

_____

_____

_____

_____

_____

_____

_____

_____

_____

_____

Practical Steps to a Well Cared-For Garden

(Pages 65-66 of *"Growing Together"*)

1. Make it your habit to remind yourself that God is the third party of your covenant private garden experience.

2. Be sensitive to your spouse's emotional and physical condition.

3. Find ways to make your spouse feel special.

4. Give respect and affection at other times.

5. Bring patience with you into the marriage bed.

6. Give your tenderness freely.

7. Let your goal be to please your spouse.

8. Always be gentle, never harsh.

9. Give no place to pain or force.

10. Give complete deference and respect to your spouse's inhibitions.

11. Determine what you both enjoy and explore its boundaries. It is worth repeating; govern this with deference and respect.

12. Do something to make the garden setting special.

13. Do what is necessary to make yourself inviting and attractive to your mate.

14. Be aware of little distractions and tensions.

    (Song of Solomon 2:15a NKJV) "Catch us the foxes, The little foxes that spoil the vines,"

15. Make it your habit to remind yourself that God is the third party of your covenant private garden experience. (Step 1 bears repeating.)

Choose what you believe are the five most important of these fifteen steps in any marriage. Arrange them in order of importance. Then, in only one sentence each, explain your answers. (It's not easy to do!)

1. _____
   _____
   _____
   _____

2. _____
   _____
   _____
   _____

3. _____
   _____
   _____
   _____

4. _____
   _____
   _____
   _____

5. _____
   _____
   _____
   _____

The Second Garden: The Altar

On Page 67 of *"Growing Together,"* you read, "There is absolutely nothing more vital to a Christian married couple than shared prayer. It re-creates the conditions in the Garden of Eden before the fall. When you pray as husband and wife, your most inward thoughts, needs, and weaknesses are exposed and presented to God (and each other)."

How does prayer with your spouse reveal your inward thoughts, needs, and weaknesses?

_____

_____

_____

_____

_____

_____

Are there times when you pray with your spouse, that holding back your thoughts, needs, and weaknesses would be the right thing to do? Why, or why not?

_____

_____

_____

_____

_____

At the bottom of Page 67 of *"Growing Together,"* you read, "Praying together has two vital effects. First, praying together about circumstances and problems helps to remove their power to affect your relationship adversely. It builds bridges over the gaps that would divide you. If there are problems with anything you face, praying together will allow you to hear from God and go forward unhindered. Second, praying together provides enriching nourishment for your marriage relationship. Sharing times of prayer opens the door to *"Growing Together.""*

From these thoughts, we can conclude that there is power in praying together as husband and wife. Doing so is a bridge-builder and opens doors to moving together past your hindrances. Without a consistent prayer life, there is a lack of power, which limits the possibilities for growth in your marriage. Praying together is the soil from which marriage enrichment grows.

Be completely honest with your answers to the following questions.

Does it matter which spouse initiates and which leads prayer?

_____
_____
_____
_____

How can prayer be a time of blessing and not an inconvenience or an uncomfortable time to be avoided?

_____
_____
_____
_____
_____
_____
_____
_____

Share your thoughts with your spouse, facilitator and group. (Remember our basic boundaries for group discussions. Do not share anything personal about your husband or wife.)

On Pages 69-71 of *"Growing Together,"* there is a sample prayer. It is derived from the principles the Apostle Paul prayed in Colossians 1:9-10. Write at least another full paragraph that you could add to this prayer.

Additions to the prayer:

_____

_____

_____

_____

_____

_____

_____

_____

_____

_____

_____

_____

_____

_____

_____

_____

_____

_____

_____

_____

_____

_____

_____

_____

_____

Look at your puzzle diagram once again. Is there anything you now would change… or is there another piece you might want to add? Do so now.

Core Principles of Marriage Enrichment

1. 2. 3. 4. 5.

6. New Piece ?

Explain any changes or additions.
_____
_____
_____
_____
_____
_____
_____
_____
_____
_____
_____
_____
_____
_____
_____
_____
_____
_____
_____
_____
_____

We will not work with the puzzle again until the final chapter. You are now ready to proceed to the next chapter. Read Chapter 6 of "*Growing Together.*" Do the assignments you will find on Pages 45-54 of this workbook. If you are part of a group, there will be additional parts of the workbook to fill in at the meeting.

PART II

GOD'S LOVE AND YOUR HEARTS

Chapter 6 - WHAT IS LOVE?

On Page 75 of *"Growing Together,"* St. Augustine's words were quoted describing the love relationship among the divine Trinity.

> *"...love involves a lover, a beloved, and a spirit of love between the lover and the loved. The Father might be likened to the lover; the Son to the loved one, and the Holy Spirit is the Spirit of love."*[2]

Augustine's words illustrate love's unique, primary characteristics. They show that it is relational in its quality and function, and in its simplest form, is a connection. Those sharing it have a common, unified resolve to give to each other. There are four characteristics of love, from Augustine's words, that we can apply to marriage.

1. Love is a shared effort. It is not the responsibility of one partner alone to maintain the relationship. Both must be involved.

2. Loving agreement between husband and wife is an expression of wholeness in the marriage. Without this wholeness, their ability to function as a couple would take on limits. Each is responsible to stay in agreement, making the connection strong, and complete.

3. The Father, Son and Holy Spirit are our examples. Their love connection is completely spiritual and not in any way controlled by things carnal. In marriage, the spiritual must always be given priority over the carnal.

4. God's love has been deliberately spilled out on us. Page 76 of the book applies this to our covenant marriage connections: "God's kind of love in marriage goes beyond the borders of its covenant relationship to flow into the lives of others within its reach."

Carefully consider the exercises on the following page. Do them with an open heart and a willingness to examine your own motives and actions.

1. Do you have any attitudes that are one-sided? Do you have expectations and demands that cause problems for your spouse? Give a simple

---

[2] Augustine's writings quoted from "The Relational Disciple," © 2010 Joel Comiskey. Published by CCS Publishing, Moreno Valley, CA, P. 38.

explanation of how you might change them. It would be good to reinforce your answers with appropriate Scripture.

_____
_____
_____
_____
_____
_____
_____
_____
_____

We all have room to improve the quality of our relationships. Go back and take another look at the exercise above.

Did this exercise touch a nerve? Describe any negative feelings you had.

_____
_____
_____
_____
_____
_____
_____
_____

2. On the next page, describe any limits on your personal ability to have a healthy, whole and satisfying relationship. This exercise is intended for self-examination, not accusation. Share your thoughts with your spouse, facilitator and group. (Remember our basic boundaries for group discussions. Do not share anything personal about your husband or wife.)

_____
_____
_____
_____
_____

As before, if you have written nothing, go back and take another attempt at the exercise.

3. Agreement in marriage is vital. What are some issues that might be difficult for a husband and wife to agree on? Why?

_____
_____
_____
_____

What are some of the easier issues about which a husband and wife can agree?

_____
_____
_____
_____

4. In one sentence, describe a single characteristic of marriage that has the most positive effect on others (family, friends, etc.).

_____
_____

Now, consider characteristics of a relationship that might cause friends or family to have feelings of discomfort. If so, describe them and provide suggestions for how these can be changed. You may find it useful to back your suggestions with Scripture.

The Principle of Increase

The Bible is clear. Love is not an option. It is a commandment. On the bottom paragraph on Page 77 of *"Growing Together,"* Dr. Abramson writes that agape love "is one of the most clearly communicated commands in the New Testament. It comes directly from Jesus. As we grow together in marriage, we ought to increasingly display this love to each other." He is driving home the point that for a marriage to be successful, and for it to thrive, grow and be enriched, some things must increase. This increase must be progressive and ongoing. Many of us are familiar with these words spoken by John the Baptist, concerning Jesus.

(John 3:30 NKJV) "He must increase, but I must decrease."

We know John the Baptist was talking about his role as a recognizable figure in God's plan of salvation, and that his relative importance would decrease as Jesus' increased. When considering the marriage covenant, we can apply this same principle. Some things in us must become less, so the things from God can become more in our marriages. We can look at this in the following manner. Some of our naturally sourced thinking must decline, so our supernaturally sourced thinking can increase, and begin to have a profoundly enriching effect on our marriages. With this in mind, consider the following:

48.

1. Which of the typical negative ways you react to your spouse should change or decrease, so your marriage can experience enrichment?

_____

_____

_____

_____

_____

_____

_____

_____

2. Which of your positive attitudes should increase?

_____

_____

_____

_____

_____

_____

3. Your ability to be an encouraging spouse, who consistently enriches the marriage experience, depends on your ability to walk in godly character. What is there about your character that should decrease or increase? Think about this carefully. Be honest with yourself.

Decrease: _____

_____

_____

_____

_____

_____

_____

Increase:

_____

_____

_____

_____

_____

_____

_____

Share your thoughts with your spouse, facilitator and group. (Remember our basic boundaries for group discussions. Do not share anything personal about your husband or wife.)

The Principle of Increase in Your Marriage

The quality of your marriage is directly proportional to the quality of your character. When the quality of the marriage partners' character increases, their marriage experience deepens. It is enriched and grows stronger.

Counterfeit Love - What Love is <u>Not</u>

On Page 78 of *"Growing Together,"* Dr. Abramsons writes, "God built us to thrive on His kind of love. It is part of how He originally designed us. At times, however, we fail to understand its value. There are those of us who simply do not know how to love, or be loved. Some of us are just not equipped for it. We use the word "love" in many ways, with many implied meanings. We say, *"I love you,"* or *"I love pizza,"* or *"I love to swim,"* or *"I love reading."* Those may all be true statements, but they do not pertain to God's kind of *"agape"* love." On the following pages of *"Growing Together,"* there are three counterfeit examples of what we commonly refer to as love." Now turn to the exercises on the following pages of this workbook, relating to the subject of counterfeit love.

FIRST COUNTERFEIT: LOVE IS A SERIES OF UNCONTROLLABLE FEELINGS.

This first counterfeit for love involves a series of intense, uncontrollable feelings, such as infatuation, lust or an unhealthy need to be wanted. Its victim is driven on an emotional search to replace feelings of emptiness within. Inevitably, these counterfeit feelings will fail to satisfy. They may disguise themselves and fool the person, but will not bring long-term peace and assurance.

Do your feelings about your spouse ever seem to be out of control? Do your reactions toward your spouse reflect this? If so, comment on this. Share your thoughts with your spouse, facilitator and group.

_____

_____

_____

_____

_____

_____

_____

_____

_____

_____

Discuss remedies for this first counterfeit with your spouse, facilitator and group. (Remember our basic boundaries for group discussions. Do not share anything personal about your husband or wife.)

SECOND COUNTERFEIT: LOVE IS A SERIES OF INTENSE CONTROLLING FEELINGS.

On Page 80 of *"Growing Together,"* you read, "There are those marriages in which one or both partners find themselves being controlled by their spouse's feelings, such as jealousy, envy or a need to dominate and control."

These feelings are like a rudder, emotionally steering their partner's reactions and controlling his or her life. This second counterfeit is described as "...like being in a boat in a fast moving river, without oars, motor or anchor. Someone or something else has the rudder. It seemed right to begin with, but now its direction and speed are wrong. There appears to be no way to get it to where it would be a blessing. Its momentum appears impossible to stop, and the damage is in the process of being done. This too, is not God's kind of love."

What are some ways that a spouse might selfishly dictate the rhythm of their partner's emotional life? Share your thoughts with your spouse, facilitator and group. (Remember our basic boundaries for group discussions. Do not share anything personal about your husband or wife.)

_____

_____

_____

_____

_____

Discuss constructive steps to remedy this with your spouse, facilitator and group. If something sparks a lot of conversation, address it below.

_____

_____

_____

_____

THIRD COUNTERFEIT: LOVE IS BOTH UNCONTROLLABLE AND CONTROLLING FEELINGS.

(WORKING AT THE SAME TIME TO DESTROY WHAT GOD HAS PUT TOGETHER)

Page 80 of *"Growing Together"* refers to this third counterfeit, in which feelings are both uncontrollable and controlling. "These feelings have one or both spouses trapped in the misfortune of experiencing the worst of our two previous examples, combined. The marriage is tangled in feelings and experiences that rob it of peace and impose a sense of helplessness and emotional damage. The couple become like puppets on a string, trapped in a relationship that is out of control."

This is the classic example of both marriage partners feeding off each other's sinful attitudes and behaviors. They have woven a complicated web. What do you think is the toughest element of this to overcome?

_____

_____

_____

_____

_____

What do you think is the best way to go beyond this third counterfeit and find the path to marriage health and enrichment?

_____

_____

_____

_____

Share your answers with your spouse, facilitator and group. As always, openness with your spouse is a solid policy that will lead to marriage enrichment. Be sure to do what you can to increase your ability, and opportunity to communicate well together.

THE REMEDY

Page 81 of *"Growing Together,"* tells us, "These three counterfeit experiences of what the world calls love can be remedied by applying the simple, truthful definition of love…" Dr. Abramson gives what he calls "the proper, accurate assessment of the remedy." He says it is "straight from the Apostle Paul's hand and the Holy Spirit's heart."

"Love never fails…" (1 Corinthians 13:8a NKJV)

The paraphrase of 1 Corinthians 13:8a is revealing, *"When God's kind of love defines your marriage, it never fails."* Again, consider this definition of God's kind of love.

> "In its simplest form, it is a connection between those sharing a common, unified resolve to give to each other, regardless of what it may personally cost them."

The key then, is to give to each other whatever is necessary to enrich the marriage experience, <u>regardless of personal cost</u>. The Apostle Paul wrote the following.

> *(Philippians 2:3 NKJV) "Let nothing be done through selfish ambition or conceit, but in lowliness of mind let each esteem others better than himself."*

When you esteem your spouse's needs above your own, you position your marriage relationship for progressive enrichment. Your sacrifice brings results that not only please your spouse, but also bring favorable results to you. Practice this principle and you will change the nature of your marriage relationship from good to very good… and ultimately to great!

Discuss Philippians 2:3 with your spouse, facilitator and group. Then practice it in your marriage. You will know the boundless blessings of God's kind of love.

You are now ready to proceed to the next chapter. Read Chapter 7 of *"Growing Together."* Do the assignments you will find on Pages 55-62 of this workbook. If you are part of a group, there will be additional parts of the workbook to fill in at the meeting.

Chapter 7 - TENDER MERCIES

(Colossians 3:14 NKJV) "Therefore, as the elect of God, holy and beloved,
put on tender mercies…"

On Pages 83-84, Dr. Abramson writes, "Marriage enrichment depends on their consistent ability to keep their hearts soft toward each other… Mercies are not really tender mercies unless they are defined by tenderness of heart and its corresponding actions." This chapter advises us of a number of ways to keep our hearts soft toward our spouses. Let's look at them.

1. YOUR TENDER MERCIES TAKE DELIBERATE, LOVING ACTION TO BLESS YOUR SPOUSE IN EVERY SITUATION.

   (Ruth 2:8-9 NKJV) "…You will listen, my daughter, will you not? Do not go to glean in another field, nor go from here, but stay close by my young women. {9} Let your eyes be on the field which they reap, and go after them. Have I not commanded the young men not to touch you? And when you are thirsty, go to the vessels and drink from what the young men have drawn."

Boaz shows us that when we encounter a person who is vulnerable, it presents us with an opportunity to know if we really have tender mercies in our hearts. Boaz shielded Ruth from the dangers she would have faced gleaning in the fields. His words and actions reflected his heart.

Examine your daily interaction with your spouse. Search your heart. Is there a time when you typically ignore or fail to recognize your spouse's vulnerability? When does this occur?

_____

_____

_____

_____

_____

What deliberate action could you take, that you do not normally do, to insure that your marriage partner is insulated from hurtful things? This may be to protect your spouse from outside influences or simply to change the patterns of your words (or lack of words) and deeds to reflect the tender mercies of your heart. Be sure you do not overlook anything.

_____

_____

_____

_____

_____

_____

_____

What deliberate loving action could you take that would bless your spouse?

_____

_____

_____

_____

_____

_____

_____

_____

2. YOUR TENDER MERCIES CAN BE YOUR REFUSAL TO TAKE ADVANTAGE OF YOUR SPOUSE.

On Page 86 of *"Growing Together,"* it says, "On the threshing floor, Boaz knew Ruth was fully vulnerable to him. However, his only thoughts were to do what was right in the sight of the Lord. In that moment, his heart was soft toward her. His response was tender and gentle. He did what was best for her. It was a display of pure, tender mercies."

How do you keep your heart soft toward your spouse?

—————————————————————————————
—————————————————————————————
—————————————————————————————
—————————————————————————————
—————————————————————————————

What can you do to make your responses toward your spouse more tender and gentle?

—————————————————————————————
—————————————————————————————
—————————————————————————————
—————————————————————————————
—————————————————————————————

Can you suggest a way that helps both of you to work together to avoid hardening your hearts?

—————————————————————————————
—————————————————————————————
—————————————————————————————
—————————————————————————————
—————————————————————————————

3. YOUR TENDER MERCIES SEE YOUR SPOUSE AS PRECIOUS AND BEYOND EARTHLY VALUE.

On Page 87 of *"Growing Together,"* it says, "Joseph's example teaches us that tenderness of heart is sacrificial and protective of our spouses. He tenderly cared for Mary without regard to what anybody might have said. He knew what a precious gift she was to him and treated her accordingly. He freely gave tender mercies."

What are some ways a person can express to their spouse how precious they are to them?

_____

_____

_____

_____

_____

_____

_____

4. YOUR TENDER MERCIES REMAIN GENTLE AND UNCHANGING, EVEN WHEN YOU ARE CRITICIZED OR ATTACKED.

At the bottom of Page 87 of *"Growing Together,"* it says, "In every marriage there are conflicts. We have moments of misunderstanding and times we say things to hurt one another. In these instances, tenderness reacts as if it was a big cushion or sponge. It absorbs the attack in love." Your marriage can be greatly enriched in times of tension and stress between each other, if you will react with gentleness. Let God's kind of love assume dominion over the emotions of the moment.

How can you surrender your heart to God's love, when you find it seemingly captive to anger, disappointment or unpleasantness?

_____

_____

_____

_____

_____

_____

_____

Review this diagram once more. (Page 30 of the workbook)

"LISTENING AFTER THE SPIRIT"
(THE RIGHT WAY TO LISTEN)

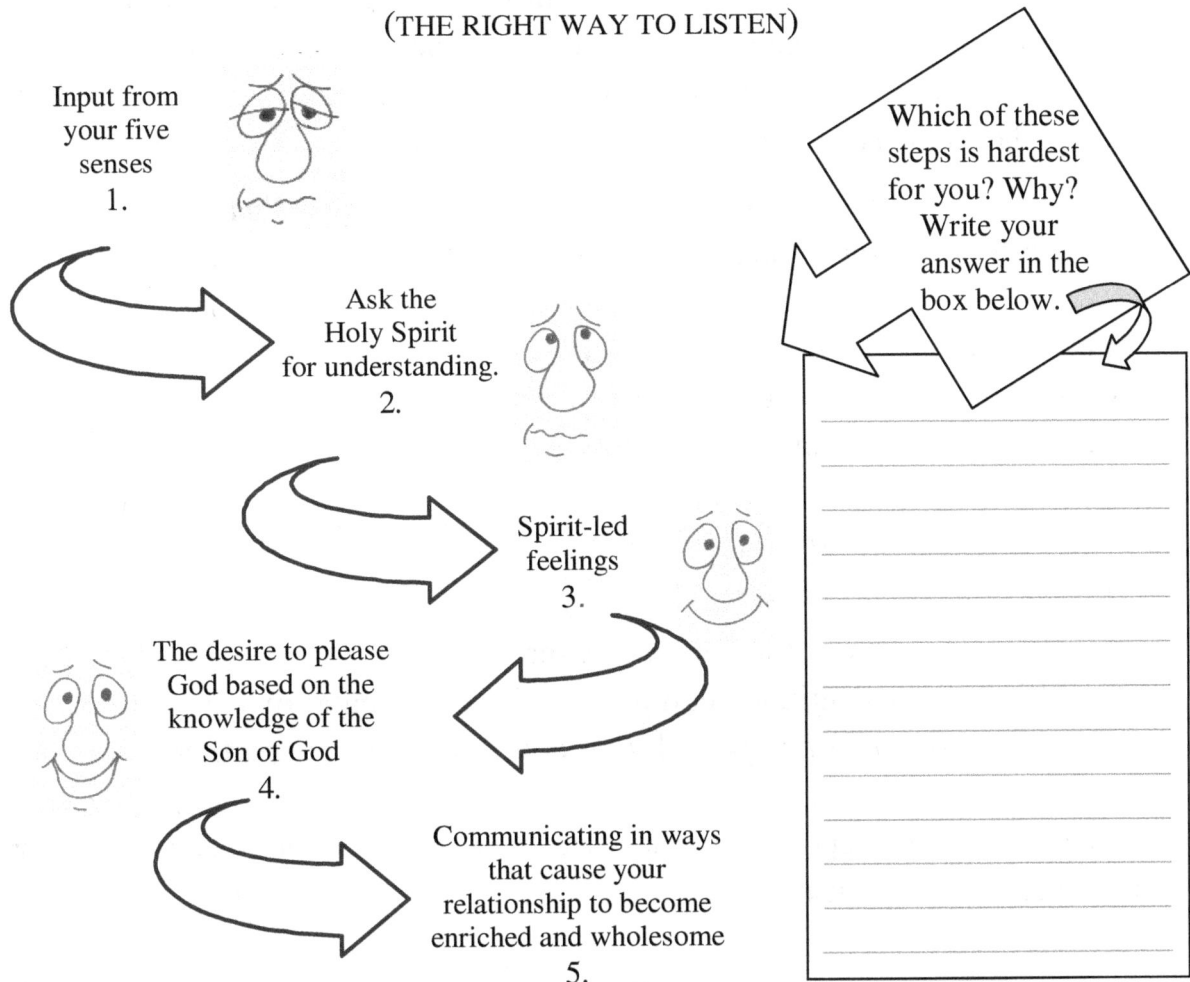

Input from
your five
senses
1.

Ask the
Holy Spirit
for understanding.
2.

Spirit-led
feelings
3.

The desire to please
God based on the
knowledge of the
Son of God
4.

Communicating in ways
that cause your
relationship to become
enriched and wholesome
5.

Which of these
steps is hardest
for you? Why?
Write your
answer in the
box below.

Can you see how important the third Person of your marriage covenant is to success and enrichment in your marriage?

(Romans 8:14 International Children's Bible) "The true children of God are those who let God's Spirit lead them."

We could re-title this diagram to read as follows:

LISTENING AND LOVING AFTER THE SPIRIT IS THE RIGHT WAY TO ENRICH YOUR MARRIAGE.

59.

5. YOUR TENDER MERCIES ARE COVERING AND QUIETING ACTS.

On Page 88 of *"Growing Together"* it says, "Your tender mercies should always watch out for ways to shield or cover your spouse from ridicule, embarrassment or shame… embrace your spouse with God's kind of reassuring love." This can be done with a simple hug or touch, and as Jesus did in the storm on the sea, by speaking a few well-chosen words.

(Mark 4:39 NKJV) "Then He arose and rebuked the wind, and said to the sea, "Peace, be still!" And the wind ceased and there was a great calm."

You can do the same. A few well-chosen, gentle words, spoken in love to your spouse, will always bring an infusion of peace. Your marriage partner, and your relationship will be enriched and strengthened.

On Page 89 of *"Growing Together,"* you read the following. Reflect on these thoughts:

"Tender mercies are the ultimate expression of Christ as our Good Shepherd… Your ultimate call as a Christian husband or wife is to be the expression of Christ toward your covenant marriage partner."

Discuss with your spouse, facilitator and group what this means for your attitudes toward your marriage.

Recap

Page 83 of the book says, "The hearts of a husband and wife can be anything from extremely hard and darkened toward one another, to soft and pliable, shining with the tender mercies of God's kind of love. Marriage enrichment depends on their consistent ability to keep their hearts soft toward each other."

On the next page is a recap of the five ways to help you keep your heart soft toward your spouse. Look again at them.

1. YOUR TENDER MERCIES TAKE DELIBERATE, LOVING ACTION TO BLESS YOUR SPOUSE IN EVERY SITUATION.

2. YOUR TENDER MERCIES CAN BE YOUR REFUSAL TO TAKE ADVANTAGE OF YOUR SPOUSE.

3. YOUR TENDER MERCIES SEE YOUR SPOUSE AS PRECIOUS AND BEYOND EARTHLY VALUE.

4. YOUR TENDER MERCIES REMAIN GENTLE AND UNCHANGING, EVEN WHEN YOU ARE CRITICIZED OR ATTACKED.

5. YOUR TENDER MERCIES ARE COVERING AND QUIETING ACTS.

Attempt to list these five in their order of relevance and importance to your covenant marriage relationship.

Now explain why your most relevant and important pick found its way from your heart to the top of the list. Discuss the list and your answer with your spouse, facilitator and group. Then have a general discussion about tender mercies. (Remember our basic boundaries for group discussions. Do not share anything personal about your husband or wife.)

These exercises should have caused you to consider many things. Write your reflections on this chapter, below. Share them with your spouse, facilitator and group.

_____
_____
_____
_____
_____
_____
_____
_____
_____
_____
_____
_____
_____
_____
_____
_____
_____
_____
_____
_____
_____
_____

You are now ready to proceed to the next chapter. Read Chapter 8 of *"Growing Together."* Do the assignments you will find on Pages 63-70 of this workbook. If you are part of a group, there will be additional parts of the workbook to fill in at the meeting.

Chapter 8 - TRUSTING HEARTS

Chapter 8 begins on Page 91 with the following paragraph:

"Trusting one another is vital to every marriage. Trust, like so many of the issues already presented, rests in the hearts of both husband and wife. Mutual trust is the glue that holds them in agreement and keeps them comfortable and confident in their oneness. Therefore, mutual trust must operate unchallenged in their hearts. When trust is compromised, it rocks the foundations of the relationship. If one spouse loses trust in the other, things destabilize. The marriage, as a covenant institution of blessing, will falter. Without trust, the wholeness of the marriage begins to come apart. It wobbles and staggers in weakness, and wavers toward the edge of failure."

List three key issues that directly affect why trust is so foundational to the relationship between marriage partners. Do so in only one sentence for each key issue. Note their order of importance in the right hand column.

	KEY ISSUES	ORDER OF IMPORTANCE
1.		
2.		
3.		

Discuss your answers, and especially the order of importance, with your spouse, facilitator and group.

Review the following two diagrams and quote found on Page 92 of *"Growing Together."*

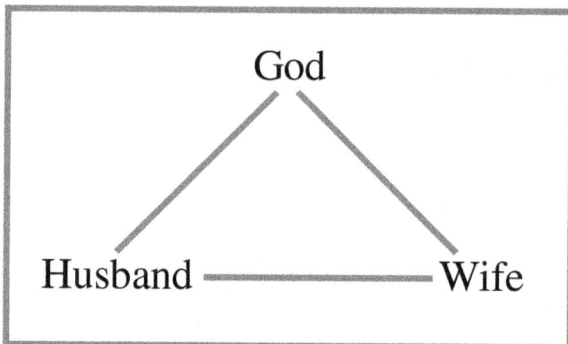

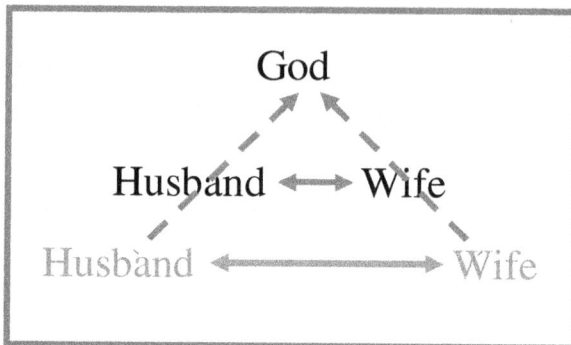

"Trust between husband and wife gathers strength and staying power when both spouses allow their faith to draw them closer to God. As they move closer to God, they move closer to each other."

Now let's look at a third diagram. You can clearly see that it is equally as revealing. Notice the direction of the arrows as trust between husband and wife loses its strength and staying power.

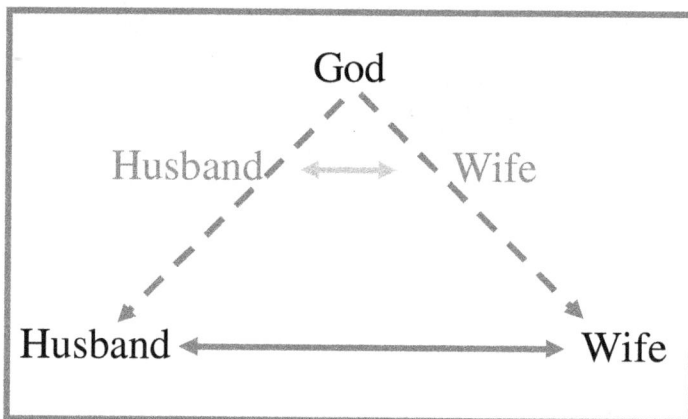

When one or both spouses pull away from God, they will inevitably be pulled away from each other. How do these diagrams and the lessons they hold relate to the chart on the previous page?

TRUSTING HEARTS DISCERN THE BEST IN THE MIDST OF
WHAT APPEARS TO BE THE WORST.

On Page 94 of *"Growing Together,"* it says, "Discernment provides you with the ability to see the truth when things appear, according to your natural thinking, to be otherwise." Trust is a decision you make in spite of how things appear. The importance of trust cannot be discounted when it comes to marriage enrichment. If you cannot discern what is really happening (if you cannot read between the lines), then you may misunderstand the intentions or actions of your spouse. When this happens, you grow apart and enable the effects of our third diagram on the previous page to take hold.

On Page 40 of the book it says, *""Growing Together"* requires that, through Christ, you believe the best in each other and expect it to come to pass." In 1 Corinthians 13:7, the Apostle Paul wrote, *"Love... hopes all things, endures all things."* Reflect on the importance of endurance to a marriage. God expects us to take the journey all the way to the finish line. With completion comes fruitfulness and blessings.

TRUSTING HEARTS PUT MEMORIES TO REST AND MOVE
AHEAD TO GOD'S BEST.

Among the most difficult things for us to overcome are emotional boundaries that were established by past experiences. These can have a controlling affect, limiting the richness of our relationships. They can breed fear, based on a previous bad relationship or experience. They can overly influence us with an unfair, unfortunate spirit of comparison. We can dwell too often and too long on what was, might have been, could have been or perhaps, even what should have been. On Page 95 of *"Growing Together,"* it says, "God wants to do a *"new thing"* in your lives. He will do this *"new thing"* if you avoid the temptation to keep looking back at what was, or might have been."

65.

Often the only way to eliminate issues from the past that would decay or destroy the richness of your marriage is to stand on your decision to trust each other, no matter what. Answer these two questions. First, what do people revisit from the past that affects their ability to trust? Second, what are three remedies from Scripture that can be put into action? Share your thoughts with your spouse, facilitator and group. (Remember our basic boundaries for group discussions. Do not share anything personal about your husband or wife.)

Things from the past that can affect someone's ability to trust:

Three remedies from Scripture:

1.

2.

3.

TRUSTING HEARTS ARE TRUSTWORTHY HEARTS.

A TRUSTWORTHY HUSBAND
(There is no higher example than the Lord.)
(Pages 96-97 of *"Growing Together"*)

(Jeremiah 31:31-32 NKJV) "Behold, the days are coming, says the LORD, when I will make a new covenant with the house of Israel and with the house of Judah; {32} not according to the covenant that I made with their fathers in the day that I took them by the hand to lead them out of the land of Egypt, My covenant which they broke, though I was a husband to them, says the LORD."

This section of Chapter 8 invites you to look at God's words describing Himself as a Husband. Eight points are listed on Pages 96-97 of *"Growing Together."* If you are a husband, select the point that speaks to you most. If you are a wife, select what speaks to you about your husband's strongest point. Explain why you picked it and how it regularly contributes to the enrichment of your marriage.

The strongest point among the eight: _____

_____

_____

_____

_____

Husbands only please: Select what you believe is your weakest point. Elaborate on why it falls into this category?

My weakest point among the eight: _____

_____

_____

_____

Husbands only please: How could you improve <u>both</u> your strongest point and weakest point, so your spouse is blessed and your marriage enriched?

I can improve my strongest point by...

_____

_____

_____

_____

I can improve my weakest point by...

_____

_____

_____

_____

_____

Discuss these four answers with your spouse, facilitator and group. (Remember our basic boundaries for group discussions. Do not share anything personal about your husband or wife.)

A TRUSTWORTHY WIFE
(Our example - the Proverbs 31 woman)
(Pages 97-98 of *"Growing Together"*)

(Proverbs 31:10-12 NKJV) "Who can find a virtuous wife? For her worth is far above rubies. {11} The heart of her husband safely trusts her; So he will have no lack of gain. {12} She does him good and not evil All the days of her life."

On Page 97 of *"Growing Together,"* it says, "The Proverb tells us, *"the heart of her husband safely trusts her."* He bases his trust on his first-hand knowledge of her character." Wives need to be acutely aware of the importance to God, and to their husbands of them having uncompromising

68.

character. A husband needs to value a closely maintained and enriched relationship with his wife. He can firmly trust in the blessings of being married to her, *"whose worth is far above rubies."*

Wives only please: What is the strongest point of your character?

_____

_____

_____

_____

_____

Wives only please: Are you aware of any weaknesses?

_____

_____

_____

_____

_____

Wives only please: What can you do to strengthen any of these weaknesses?

_____

_____

_____

_____

_____

On Page 98 of *"Growing Together,"* it says, "When hearts are equally open and trusting toward each other, there is no room for mistrust. Both husband and wife see each other as trustworthy. They are affirmed in their relationship and able to continue *"Growing Together"* in their threefold covenant with God."

This would be a great time to remind yourselves as a married couple that you are also permanently committed to the third Party of your marriage covenant, God Himself. These exercises should have caused you to consider many things. Write your reflections on this chapter, below. Share them with your spouse, facilitator and group. (Remember our basic boundaries for group discussions. Do not share anything personal about your husband or wife.)

You are now ready to proceed to the final chapter. Read Chapter 9 of *"Growing Together."* Do the assignments you will find on Pages 71-72 of this workbook.

Chapter 9 - FOR THE GLORY OF GOD

Page 100 of *"Growing Together"* sums up the challenge for your marriage relationship:

> "The book has offered you ways to understand and secure your relationship. Your marriage gathers its strengths from your agreement and oneness, as you journey to your destiny together. You are joined with each other, going somewhere… to the glory of God."

We will finish the workbook with a review of the principles listed on Pages 100-101 of *"Growing Together."*

- ☑ Your relationship is a God idea.
- ☑ You are joined in a holy covenant with God. Live your lives before Him in the knowledge that He is always with you.
- ☑ Marriage is a partnership of grace.
- ☑ God made husband and wife different by deliberate design.
- ☑ Honor Christ by submitting to each other.
- ☑ God has given you Seven Pillars of Love upon which to build your marriage.
- ☑ Speaking the Truth in Love is a key to your closeness and success.
- ☑ Listening "After the Spirit" pleases God and enriches your marriage.
- ☑ Forgiveness shuts the door on the devil and keeps the damage from your doorstep.
- ☑ Physical intimacy in marriage is a God idea.
- ☑ You will be blessed with two private gardens in your marriage, the marriage bed and the prayer garden. Tend them with care and value them with honor.
- ☑ Prayer is the most intimate and powerful thing you can do together.
- ☑ God's kind of love never fails.
- ☑ Tender mercies are a vital part of *"Growing Together."*

☑ View your marriage as an instrument to reveal the glory of God to all it touches.

We conclude with this final principle.

☑ Walk a righteous path together. You will be blessed as God honors and enriches your lives.

Your final assignments are to meditate on these fifteen principles and have a meaningful discussion with your spouse, your facilitator and group. Then, take one more attempt at your puzzle. See if anything has changed now that you have completed the workbook. Share what you have learned and how your heart has been softened by reading *"Growing Together,"* and working your way through the pages of this workbook.

Core Principles of Marriage Enrichment

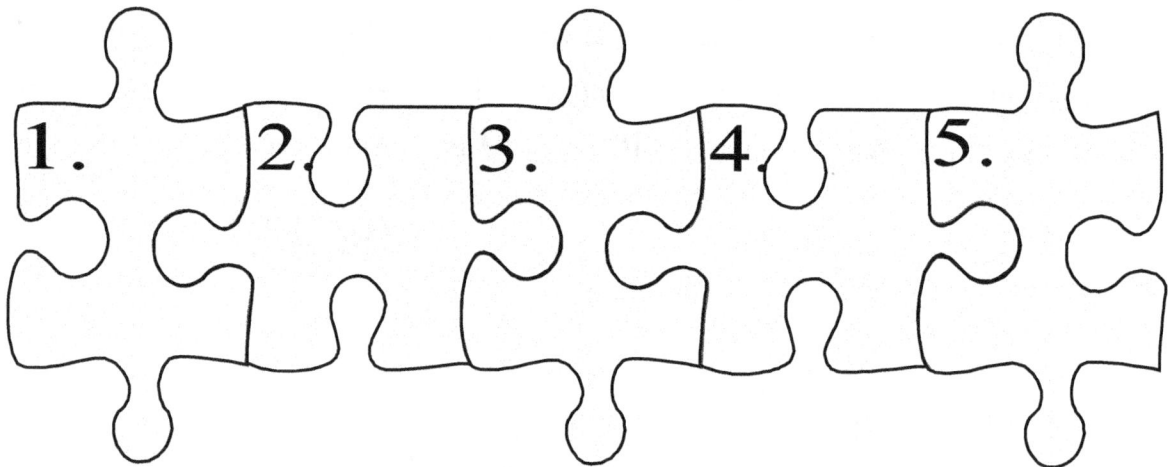

1.   2.   3.   4.   5.

With every blessing, "Growing Together" in Christ,

Dr. Bob and Nancy Abramson

Dr. Bob Abramson

Dr. Abramson has extensive experience in cross-cultural marriage issues. He and his wife Nancy have pastored multicultural, international churches in New York City and the Fiji Islands in the South Pacific. He also established or taught in Bible schools and ministry training centers in New Zealand, Fiji, Taiwan, Hong Kong, Malaysia, Europe and the United States.

Dr. Abramson has a Doctor of Ministry from Erskine Theological Seminary, with a concentration in supra-cultural marriage enrichment. He also earned a Masters in Religion from Liberty University, and a Bachelor of Arts in the Bible with a minor in Systematic Theology from Southeastern University.

Dr. Abramson and his wife Nancy live in Lake Worth, Florida. They have five grown children and five grandchildren.

If you wish to contact Dr. Abramson, please visit
www.mentoringministry.com
or
Dr.Bob@mentoringministry.com

Dr. Abramson is also the author of
"Just a Little Bit More - The Heart of a Mentor"
(Accounts of Cross-Cultural Mentoring and the Lessons they Hold)

and

The Leadership Puzzle -
Marketplace, Ministry and Life
(A Two-Workbook Series)

---

www.ingramcontent.com/pod-product-compliance
Lightning Source LLC
Chambersburg PA
CBHW080054280326
41934CB00014B/3313